THE OFFICIAL
NEWCASTLE UNITED
ANNUAL 2024

Written by Mark Hannen

Designed by Adam Wilsh

Thanks to Michael Bolam, Paul Joannou, Joe Nelson and Issy Reid.

D1612680

A Grange Publication

© 2023. Published by Grange Communications Ltd., Edinburgh, under licence from Newcastle United Football Club. Printed in the EU.

Photographs © Serena Taylor, Getty Images & Alamy Live News.

ISBN 978-1-915879-26-4

WELCOME

Welcome to the Official Newcastle United Annual 2024.

Last season proved to be a truly memorable campaign. To rise from bottom of the Premier League in November 2021 to finish fourth 18 months later was an incredible achievement and we hope many of you were able to relive the season through the Amazon Prime documentary.

Throw in a Wembley cup final, which you can read about further on in the Annual, and it just gives us all the appetite for more which we will be doing our utmost to achieve this season.

We would also like to thank you the supporters, young and old, for the continued phenomenal backing you give the team home and away, our progress could not have been achieved without you on board.

This season of course brings the challenge (and excitement) of Champions League football for the first time in 21 years. Hosting the cream of Europe at St. James' Park is sure to create more wonderful moments in our history.

A word too for our Women, who won their league last year, have recently turned professional and, like our men, are aiming high once again this season.

We're all looking forward to a very exciting future for Newcastle United and we're thrilled you're with us for the ride.

Enjoy the read, which once again brings you so much action and colour from Newcastle United.

Howay the lads and lasses.

CONTENTS

IMAGES FROM THE
2022/23 SEASON

It's all very light-hearted as the lads prepare for the annual team photograph.

We're off to Qatar! England internationals Callum Wilson, Nick Pope and Kieran Trippier.

The lads and lasses at the Great North Children's Hospital before they began their rounds of the wards last Christmas.

The club held monthly Memory Café's at St. James' Park, helping those with dementia. Here legends Bob Moncur and Malcolm Macdonald hold court.

United may have lost the match on the pitch but they won the off-field battle at Wembley and in London hands down.

Our Women's team won promotion to the Northern Premier League and here they are at their end of season awards dinner with Amanda Staveley and Mehrdad Ghodoussi.

The kit and the boots are all ready for the lads in the home team changing room.

Shay Given returned to the Benton Training Ground to put on a goalkeeping masterclass for United's current shot-stoppers.

Another brilliant display by Wor Flags, this time in the East Stand, for the last home game of the season.

Matt Ritchie, Anthony Gordon, Bruno Guimarães and Joelinton engage in a bit of Teqball at the club's revamped Training Centre.

The final group picture of the season after the Leicester game celebrating Champions League qualification.

Sam Fender entertained his fans with two sold-out shows at St. James' Park in June. What a performer!

SEASON REVIEW

Newcastle United qualified for the Champions League for the first time since 2002/03 - the undoubted highlight for what was a tremendous season for the club. After an excellent second half finish to the previous season, from January - May 2022, there was clear optimism in the air that the Magpies could take that form into the new campaign and finish at least in the top ten. What unravelled as the weeks passed was a finale much greater than even the most passionate and optimistic Geordie fan could ever have hoped for.

AUGUST

It was an early August kick off for the 2022/23 Premier League season and newly promoted Nottingham Forest, back in the top-flight after a 23-year absence, were the opening day visitors at St. James' Park. It finished 2-0 to United, Fabian Schär and Callum Wilson with second half goals, but really it could have been five or six. So, off to a flyer and only the Magpies' second opening day win in ten attempts. A 0-0 draw at Brighton followed before Champions Manchester City headed north. An epic encounter finished 3-3, a tad disappointing for the hosts who had led 3-1, but in the end a share of the spoils wasn't a bad result come the end of 90 enthralling minutes where the highlight was probably Kieran Trippier's magnificent free kick which left Ederson a statuesque figure in the Gallowgate End goal. A stunning Allan Saint-Maximin strike (awarded BBC Goal of the Month) salvaged United a point at Molineux before Eddie Howe's men suffered a heart-breaking, and undeserved, injury time defeat at Anfield on the last day of the month.

SEPTEMBER

International football meant that the Magpies only played two games in September, that after cramming five into 25 days the previous month! Whilst playing well, they couldn't turn draws into wins thus ending the month with only two points added to their tally. Both games were on Tyneside which made both draws even more disappointing. In the first encounter, a VAR decision which went against United, and was later deemed to be incorrect, meant Crystal Palace took a point back to London after a goalless stalemate. Two weeks later Bournemouth rocked up at St. James' Park and had the temerity to take the lead before Alexander Isak equalised a mere six minutes later. The Geordies had taken seven points from a possible 18 and were 11th in the league so going into October they were under a bit of pressure to turn those draws into maximum point returns - and by golly they did just that in fine style!

OCTOBER

United were down on the banks of the Thames at Fulham (many fans having travelled down the Thames by boat - the Geordie Armada) on the first day of the month, a venue where they knocked in four on their last visit in May 2021. And low and behold they repeated the trick once again, helped it has to be said by a red card dished out to home defender Nathaniel Chalobah after only eight minutes. Wilson, Miguel Almirón (2) and Sean Longstaff were all on target for the blue-clad Magpies with the Paraguayan's first, an incredible acrobatic volley into the top corner of the net. A late home goal was the only disappointment for a team that loves to deal in clean sheets. Five home goals the following Saturday against Brentford was the perfect indication United were on the move and an away draw at Old Trafford eight days later is something never to be sniffed at. Back to St. James' Park in midweek and Everton were sent packing, Almirón maintaining his rich run of goalscoring form, and that was followed by a massive 2-1 win in north London where a very inventive and opportunistic Wilson chip from 30 yards out helped earn a 2-1 winning scoreline against Tottenham. Aston Villa were crushed 4-0 at the end of the month which ended with five wins out of six for Eddie Howe and with it, the manager of the month award, his second managerial gong in his 12 months at the club.

NOVEMBER

Another month where there were only two league games played, but this time there was a legitimate reason for the inactivity at grounds up and down the country. The FIFA World Cup, somewhat controversially awarded to Qatar, had to be played in the winter months to protect the health of the players. So, for the first time in history, there was a six-week break in the middle of the majority of European club seasons. Fortunately for United they won both games which meant a buoyant squad, signed off for now, sat

in a very healthy third place in the table, behind only the eventual top two, Manchester City and Arsenal. The Magpies had certainly found their scoring touch and were in devastating form on the south coast at Southampton, running out very comfortable 4-1 winners. Chelsea were our opponents for the last game of the first half of the season and at a rocking Gallowgate, where the fans roared on United every step of the way, Joe Willock hit a superb 67th minute winner to heap more misery on Graham Potter's Blues.

DECEMBER

Lionel Messi lifted the World Cup for Argentina in a thrilling final which was eventually settled on penalties, but all the good people of Newcastle were bothered about was the resumption of the Premier League and a continuation of the form they'd shown earlier in the season. Bournemouth were beaten in the League Cup (more to come in this annual) before Boxing Day saw fans back watching what they loved the most. United were at struggling Leicester and put the game to bed in the first seven minutes with a two-goal salvo before adding a third on the half hour which meant they were on cruise control for the last hour of the game. The Magpies were back home on New Year's Eve to face 'local' rivals Leeds United where a disappointing game ended 0-0. Still, United ended the year on 34 points and in third place in the table. All in all it had been a very satisfying 2022 when you compare that to 11 points and 19th place at the end of 2021.

JANUARY

A pretty 'dry' month in terms of goals as in the three league matches played there was just one solitary goal – and that came in the 89th minute of the home win over Fulham. First up in the new year was a top of the table clash at the Emirates where title chasing Arsenal, seven points clear at the top of the table, entertained the third placed Magpies. Boasting a 100% home record, United defended stoutly to become the first team to take a point away from the Gunners' home fortress. January actually turned into London versus Newcastle as Fulham and Crystal Palace were next up for Eddie's charges. The Whites frustratingly kept United at bay until the penultimate minute of the game when Isak joyously headed home from close range to send the relieved Gallowgate enders wild. A stalemate at Selhurst Park rounded the month off but there had been four other fixtures played where a disappointing FA Cup defeat at Sheffield Wednesday was rapidly forgotten as the Geordies sealed their first League Cup Final appearance for 47 years.

FEBRUARY

February wasn't the best of months for Newcastle United; four games, no wins, defeat in the League Cup Final and a red card for goalkeeper Nick Pope which meant, very unfortunately, that he was ruled out of the Wembley showpiece occasion. West Ham were the first visitors to Tyneside and, in a below par performance, the two United's shared the spoils in a 1-1 draw, that despite the Magpies scoring as early as the third minute. Another uneventful 1-1 followed at Bournemouth seven days later before the Anfield Reds came north to Gallowgate for a match that would provide a real test for the European chasing Magpies. As it happened, in a white-hot atmosphere, the contest was all over inside 20 minutes with two Liverpool goals and United reduced to ten men with Nick Pope's sending off. That said, United weren't over run and could have remarkably scored a goal or two themselves in a surprisingly front-foot second half showing. So, come the end of the month, and following the trek back from London with no silverware to show, United had no choice but to dust themselves down, not feel sorry for themselves, and move positively on to March.

MARCH

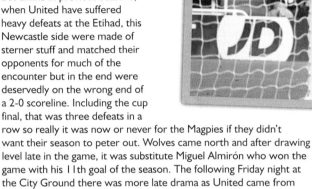

Spring began with probably United's toughest away trip of the season, a fixture against reigning Champions Manchester City who were just clicking into top form as they usually do in the title run-in. But unlike in previous seasons, when United have suffered heavy defeats at the Etihad, this Newcastle side were made of sterner stuff and matched their opponents for much of the encounter but in the end were deservedly on the wrong end of a 2-0 scoreline. Including the cup final, that was three defeats in a row so really it was now or never for the Magpies if they didn't want their season to peter out. Wolves came north and after drawing level late in the game, it was substitute Miguel Almirón who won the game with his 11th goal of the season. The following Friday night at the City Ground there was more late drama as United came from behind to win with an injury time penalty from Isak, that after what would have been a dream first goal for substitute Elliot Anderson was controversially (and wrongly) ruled out by VAR.

APRIL

April turned out to be a fantastic month for the Magpies and maybe a season-defining one. Seven games, six wins, 22 goals (eight of which Callum Wilson netted) and nicely placed in third spot in the table throughout all 30 days. The heartache of the League Cup Final defeat was swiftly erased as Erik ten Hag's side were despatched 2-0 at St. James' Park before United hit an incredible five goals on the road at West Ham. United then inflicted only a second home defeat of the season on the Bees of Brentford before a quick reality check saw a 3-0 reverse at Villa Park. But Newcastle responded in the best possible way by smashing five past Tottenham in the first 21 minutes at Gallowgate in what has to have been the most sensational opening to a game any Magpies fan has ever witnessed. The goal glut continued with four at Goodison Park, including a 'never seen before' mesmerising assist by Isak to set up a 'tap-in' for Jacob Murphy, before relegation bound Southampton were seen off on the final day of a captivating month.

MAY

Title challengers Arsenal arrived on Tyneside for the first fixture of May looking to not only avenge last season's shattering defeat which cost them a top-four finish, but to get the three points to keep their fading title hopes alive. And credit to the Gunners they did just that, but it was a game United could easily have won themselves such are the fine margins upon which Premier League games are decided. Having held third place in the table since beating Manchester United in early April, the Magpies were in no mood to let their Champions League qualification aspirations slip away, especially with Liverpool on the charge in fifth place. The equation was simple enough, seven points from the last four games would guarantee at worst a fourth-place finish. Two penalties from Callum Wilson earned a point at Leeds in Sam Allardyce's first home game, Brighton were then despatched 4-1 on Tyneside before Liverpool unexpectedly dropped two points against Aston Villa meaning a point in the final home game of the season against Leicester City would see Eddie Howe's men over the line. In a slightly nervy 0-0, which included a superb save from Nick Pope in second half injury time, that's exactly what United achieved amidst wonderful scenes at St. James' Park. A draw at Chelsea in the final game of the season, with another Geordie Armada invasion, this time 1,500 strong, meant a fourth-place finish which rounded off what had been a brilliant season for the Geordies.

FLOODLIT FOOTBALL

There is nothing better than watching football under floodlights and the special atmosphere it creates. Club Historian Paul Joannou looks at Newcastle United under the bright lights since they were first switched on back in 1953.

EARLY TESTS

Way back during Victorian times clubs around the country tried early methods of lighting up games of football in the evening. These were maybe rather primitive by modern standards, but over 100 years ago very innovative. A match under lights was played at Bramall Lane in Sheffield as early as 1878 when artificial light was powered by batteries and dynamos. Blackburn and Darwen also hosted evening games as did Third Lanark's original club, 3rd Lanark Rifle Volunteers. Here in the North East, during April 1888, Tyneside club Elswick Rangers travelled to Wearside to meet Palmer's Hill FC for 'illuminated football'. It was decades though before floodlighting really took hold in Britain.

Football's authorities allowed friendly games to take place under lights and that really started to take off after World War Two, but it was a while before Newcastle United installed a floodlighting system. In October 1951 the Magpies installed some degree of lighting at St. James' Park to allow evening training by the players. But United were way behind one or two other clubs, notably at The Dell, Southampton and Highbury home of Arsenal where floodlit friendlies had already started. Back then, one press comment noted that it is "no secret of the fact that in the years to come night-shift soccer will be the vogue". And that was very true.

Match programme from United's first floodlit game in 1953.

The club's 'telegraph-pole' lighting on Leazes Terrace.

Comments after the game with Celtic were mixed; "Spectators who watched from nearer ground level found the lighting effect extremely good, but from the press box, which was in the roof of the main stand, there were patches of shadow on the playing area." A club spokesman noted that, "from every point of view, the game with Celtic was an unqualified success".

One supporter recalled; "We entered the ground and found it all in relative darkness. There were a few small lights in the old West Stand. The ground remained in darkness until the players came out just before kick-off and only then were the lights switched on – and at the half-time break the lights were switched off, the ground was in darkness again. That was repeated at full-time, so we had to make our way out of the ground in the gloom." There were no safety rules back then! But as one report noted; "It was still a grand spectacle." Floodlit football had arrived.

Victorian floodlighting at the Oval in London 1878.

FIRST AT ST. JAMES' PARK

On 25 February 1953, United played their very first game under floodlights at St. James' Park for an attractive game against Celtic; the FA Cup winners versus Scottish Cup winners. The system consisted of small clusters of lights erected on 'telegraph poles' along the Leazes Terrace side of the ground, and on gantries high up on the main West Stand roof. Fletcher Brothers installed the system which had 80 lights of 1000 watts each. A crowd of 41,888 saw United win 2-0 with Chilean striker George Robledo hitting two goals under the new lights which were, by modern standards, far from being the bright and vivid illumination as we experience these days.

FOOTBALL LEAGUE DEBUT

Football's authorities were slow in giving sanction for league or cup matches to take place under floodlights. In the FA Cup, floodlighting for replays was allowed, and United's ground was the venue for the very first between league clubs, a Round One replay between Carlisle United and Darlington during November 1955 which the Quakers won 3-1. Football League matches were also given the green light by season 1955/56 but only for rescheduled fixtures after a postponement. When Newcastle United travelled to face Portsmouth at Fratton Park for an evening clash during February 1956, the two clubs marked the very first league meeting under floodlights. And then the system actually failed just before kick-off! Following a delay, United won that historic encounter 2-0.

Action from Fratton Park, the game's first league match under the lights.

United under the lights in October 1953 at the old Brockville Park, home of Falkirk.

THE TOWERS ARRIVE

With state-of-the-art floodlighting systems being erected around the country, Newcastle United knew they had to upgrade the inferior lighting at St. James' Park. On 26 March 1958 the club marked the installation of four giant pylons at Gallowgate by hosting the annual Football League versus Scottish League contest – back then a much-awaited clash, one step from a full international match. The Football League side won 4-1 in front of a 46,800 attendance with the lights being a massive improvement on the previous scheme at Gallowgate. A young Bobby Robson was in the League's line-up that night.

At a cost of £40,000, the pylons were over 190 feet high, the tallest in the UK and they became a Tyneside landmark for nearly 20 years. Each tower held 45 powerful arc lamps and the new system was described as, "second to none in Britain". It was a vast advance and gave splendid illumination.

More floodlit friendlies took place including a mouth-watering clash with Barcelona in August 1960 which resulted in a terrific encounter that United narrowly lost 4-3. The Black'n'Whites also saw Brazilian side Bela Vista arrive on Tyneside and receive a thrashing under the lights, losing by all of 12-1.

FLOODLIT FRIENDLIES

During the mid-to-late Fifties clubs all over the country started to play floodlight friendlies and the Magpies faced a long list of clubs from Europe and especially from Scotland, under the lights, both at St. James' Park and on their travels. Early games at Gallowgate included visitors from Austria, France, Germany and Poland while several clubs made the short trip across the border from Scotland, including Hibernian and Hearts. Pictured is action under the lights during October 1953 at the old Brockville Park, home of Falkirk. United lost that game 3-2, that match was also the first to be broadcast in Scotland.

Programme from the Football League versus Scottish League contest in 1958.

Night football against Brazilians Bela Vista.

The four giant Gallowgate pylons which dominated Tyneside's landcape.

EURO MAGIC

When United entered Europe for the first time for season 1968/69, competitive football against continental opponents brought with it very special nights under floodlights. After the Magpies had enjoyed three seasons in the Fairs Cup, by the time they had qualified for the UEFA Cup, due to ground redevelopment, three of the pylons were taken down to begin with, with a temporary smaller structure erected along with new lights on the top of the West Stand. Then once the new East Stand was erected, the pylons were gone forever. Lighting on the top of the East Stand and West Stand were switched on, featured in a UEFA Cup match against French club Bastia during November 1977 – Alan Gowling scoring in the 3-1 defeat.

Floodlight football now became the norm, especially with European competition in full flow. In the Champions League during March 2003, pictured are the Black'n'Whites entering Milan's famous San Siro beneath the lights, while the Magpies faced FC Basel in November 2003 and Shola Ameobi is pictured celebrating a goal with the bright lights of St Jakob-Park in the background.

FLOODLIGHTS FAILURE

St. James' Park suffered a rare floodlight failure in March 1977 during a league match against Ipswich Town. A North Eastern Electricity Board fault to the power grid at Newburn left Gallowgate in gloom – the first occasion that happened at the stadium. On 78 minutes the lights suddenly lost full power and the stadium was plunged into a gloomy darkness. Referee Eric Garner called the players together and decided to allow play to continue in partial light as there was only around ten minutes of the game remaining. Full power was restored just before the scheduled 90 minutes. And that was just in time for Ipswich to grab a late equaliser in a 1-1 draw.

LIGHTING TODAY

Today, United's floodlighting is right up there with the best. Meeting full UEFA guidelines there are an incredible 342 lights brightly shining onto the playing arena with a lux level of 2000. United's lighting system was upgraded in 2016 when there were only 200 lights and a much lower lux level. They are operated via an electronic ballast system for greater efficiency.

(Top) United walk onto the San Siro turf in Milan. (Middle Left) Shola Ameobi celebrates his goal in Basel, Switzerland beneath the lights. (Middle Right) Lights shine brightly as Alan Gowling scores against Bastia. (Bottom) Pop Robson hits the net against Setubal in March 1969.

St. James' Park with lighting on the stand roof.

SPOT THE BALL

Can you spot the correct ball positions in the below images from when Newcastle took on Crystal Palace and Nottingham Forest last season?

Answers on page 62

NOSTALGIA
From The 1960s & 1970s

We've recently unearthed some photographs in the club archive from the late 1960s and early 1970s. They're a fascinating insight of what life was like in and around St. James' Park some 55 years ago.

Fans waiting outside the Gallowgate End before the turnstiles open with the usual police presence.

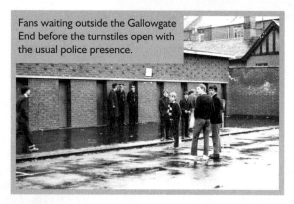

Here's the Tyne Tees TV dish which was used back in the early days of the Shoot! Programme on Sunday afternoons.

One lucky lad has just got hold of his ticket for the Fairs Cup Final back in May 1969.

This wall is opposite where the Sir Bobby Robson statue is now; young fans wait for the players to arrive in their cars.

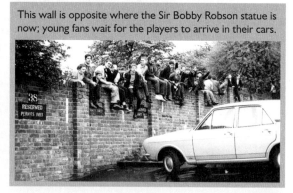

An older supporter, stood on the path on Strawberry Place, watches on as fans enter the ground through the old Gallowgate End gates.

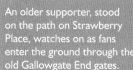

Rangers fans clamber up the Gallowgate floodlight pylon to watch the Fairs Cup semi-final second leg tie. United won 2-0.

A classic picture of a packed Leazes End, lots of younger fans at the front, the older ones stood higher up the terrace, OAPs used to stand on the right at the front.

1971 and the players are training on the cinder track around the ground - Tudor, Clark, Macdonald and Craig.

Up at the Leazes End and you can see two of the turnstile entrances on the right. There used to be huge queues there!

Back in the day many clubs put broken glass on top of brick walls to stop fans getting in the ground free of charge!

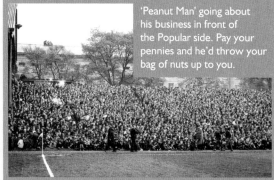

'Peanut Man' going about his business in front of the Popular side. Pay your pennies and he'd throw your bag of nuts up to you.

Fans getting advice from the constabulary operating out of their Police Box within the confines of the ground.

Looking up towards the main West Stand (now Milburn) from Strawberry Place, quite an incline still there today.

Believe it or not, fans in the Leazes End used to bring toilet rolls to the game and throw them down onto the back of the net!

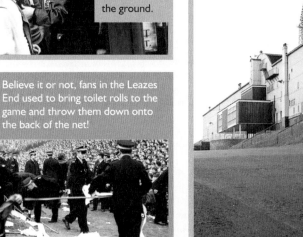

It looks like there is a bit of ticket touting going on, a very common (but illegal) practice back in the 1970s.

A very interesting aerial shot of St. James' Park in the late 1960s.

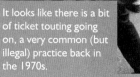

The Magpie Club, a famous gathering point for fans before and after games, situated opposite the ground on Barrack Road.

SPOT THE DIFFERENCE

Can you spot the ten differences between these two pictures of when Newcastle took on Arsenal last season?

Answers on page 62

MAGIC MOMENTS A-Z

An A-Z of some of the Greatest Moments in Newcastle United's history.

Alan Shearer scores his first United goal against Wimbledon in 1996.

Barcelona are beaten 3-2 at St. James' Park in the Champions League in 1997.

Craig Bellamy scores United's last-minute winner against Feyenoord in 2002.

Delight for Alan Shearer as he celebrates scoring goal number 206 for Newcastle in the Tyne-Wear derby in 2006.

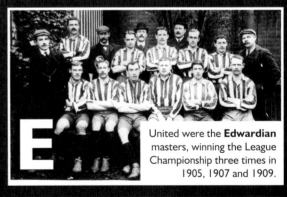

United were the **Edwardian** masters, winning the League Championship three times in 1905, 1907 and 1909.

United's first ever European game ends in a 4-0 victory over **Feyenoord**.

Alan **Gowling** scores United's goal in the 1976 League Cup Final.

H

Eddie **Howe** saves United from relegation in season 2021/22 and 12 months later leads the Magpies into the Champions League with a fourth-place finish.

I

United played out a memorable 2-2 draw in Italy with **Inter Milan** in 2003.

J

Jackie Milburn scores after 45 seconds in the 1955 FA Cup Final against Manchester City (not quite as quick as İlkay Gündoğan's for City a few months ago!).

Kevin Keegan leads United to promotion in 1984.

K

L

Len Shackleton scores six goals as United thump Newport County 13-0 in October 1946, their record victory.

M

Malcolm Macdonald scores against Burnley in one of United's most memorable FA Cup semi-final victories in 1974.

N

Newcastle East End absorb their West End rivals, taking over St. James' Park in the process and a new name is chosen in 1892 - Newcastle United.

O

Bobby Robson wins his **One** hundredth match as United boss, 4-3 versus Manchester United in 2001.

Pelé, the greatest footballer the world has ever seen, turns out against Newcastle United for his club Santos in 1972.

Q Mick **Quinn** sensationally scores four times on his United debut against Leeds in 1989.

R United pull off a stunning 5-0 UEFA Cup victory in Belgium against **Royal Antwerp** in 1994.

Jimmy **Scoular** lifts the FA Cup at Wembley, the third of United's 1950s cup victories. **S**

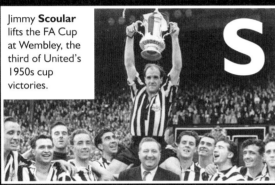

T Cheick **Tioté** scores the dramatic equaliser against Arsenal in 2011 as they come from four goals down to draw 4-4.

U **Újpest Dózsa** are beaten in 1969 and United win their first European Trophy.

Sweet **Victories**, how about the 5-0 over Manchester United in October 1996? **V**

W It was defeat at **Wembley** in 2023 but the United fans made it a day to remember.

EXtra time. One of the best was Allan Saint-Maximin scoring a stunning extra-time winner in 2020 against Oxford in the FA Cup. **X**

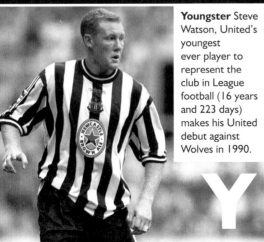

Youngster Steve Watson, United's youngest ever player to represent the club in League football (16 years and 223 days) makes his United debut against Wolves in 1990. **Y**

Z United qualify for the Champions League for the first time with a 2-2 draw against Croatia **Zagreb** in 1997.

CALLUM WILSON

Callum Wilson began his career at his hometown club Coventry City in 2009, rising through the club's academy and enjoying loan spells at Kettering and Tamworth, before scoring 23 goals in 41 senior appearances for the Sky Blues during his final season at the club in 2013/14.

After moving to AFC Bournemouth in the summer of 2014, Wilson fired the Cherries to promotion in his first season - scoring 20 goals in 45 Championship outings - before becoming the South Coast club's talisman in the Premier League.

His excellent and consistent performances brought full international recognition in November 2018. Having previously represented the England U21s, Callum scored on his England debut against the United States at Wembley in a 3-0 win for Gareth Southgate's side.

Callum moved to Tyneside in the summer of 2020 and scored on his United debut against West Ham on 12 September 2020 as United won 2-0 at the London Stadium. He was the club's top goalscorer in 2020/21 with 12 league goals and won the United Player of the Season trophy for 2020/21, narrowly pipping Allan Saint-Maximin and newcomer Joe Willock to the award.

Wilson took the famous United number 9 shirt at the start of the 2021/22 season, the tenth player to do so in the Premier League era. One of his most memorable goals was the opener against Tottenham at St. James' Park in October 2021, the first Gallowgate goal under the new ownership of the club. Sadly, a calf / Achilles injury picked up against Manchester United two months later, kept him sidelined until May 2022.

Back in the side, he scored twice at Burnley on the last day of the season taking him top of United's goalscoring charts. A goal on the opening day of the 2022/23 season against Nottingham Forest was his third in a row for United on the season's first weekend.

Part of England's 26-man squad for the 2022 World Cup in Qatar, Callum played his first World Cup game coming on as a substitute against Iran on 21 November. Wilson selflessly set up England's sixth goal for Jack Grealish against the Iranians before appearing again in the group stages in the 3-0 victory over Wales.

In April 2023 Callum scored more Premier League goals than any other player (8) but still remains shy of a United hat-trick having netted ten braces for the Magpies. His 38 Premier League goals for United [at the end of the 2022/23 season] puts him in sixth place in the all-time NUFC PL goalscorers chart. Another nine goals and Callum will move into outright second in the table behind the legendary Alan Shearer.

ELLIOT ANDERSON'S
USA DIARY

Local lad Elliot Anderson kept a diary at the PL Summer Series in July and here are his reflections on what was a very successful trip both personally and for the club.

"We were invited to compete in the Premier League Summer Series, along with five other clubs so in terms of pre-season preparation it was sure to provide us with three very competitive matches. And going out to America, well that was a tremendous experience, especially for me and the other young lads in the squad.

WEDNESDAY 19 JULY
"We'd beaten Glasgow Rangers 2-1 at Ibrox the previous night which was a terrific win, especially for the 8,000 Geordies who'd travelled up for the game. Rather than return home we flew to the United States from Glasgow the following morning and arrived at around 2pm local time in Atlanta. That night a few of the lads went off to see the Braves against the Diamondbacks and had a great time. Baseball's not a sport we know that well in England, but the Americans absolutely love it.

THURSDAY 20 JULY
"There's a huge fan base out in the States and they're just as fanatical as the supporters back home so it was great that the club held fan engagement events whilst we were out there. Here's club legends Shola Ameobi, Shay Given and Steve Harper with a group of very enthusiastic fans! Everywhere we went, in all three cities, the number of black and white shirts we saw was phenomenal.

FRIDAY 21 JULY
"Joelinton arrived a little late in the States but he didn't take long to get acquainted with the surroundings. Today was a pretty intense day of training with our first game only a couple of days away. We used the facilities at Walsh Field (Pace Academy) which were first class. The weather was really hot most of the time but we also had some pretty big downpours.

SATURDAY 22 JULY

"Time to say goodbye to Atlanta for a couple of days as we flew to Philadelphia in the afternoon after a morning of training. The schedule was full on in terms of travel but at the same time the internal flights weren't too taxing. This was a new destination for me and of course when in Philly you have to visit the Rocky Steps at the Philadelphia Museum of Art. They told us the steps, which are symbolic of the city of Philadelphia, demonstrate how you can become a champion through hard work and determination. A lesson for us all.

SUNDAY 23 JULY

"We'd worked hard on the training pitch in pretty hot conditions so the idea for the first game (Aston Villa) was that most of us would play 45 minutes each. I was in the 'first half' team so to speak and it didn't start too well, going two down in the first 11 minutes but then, just before the half hour, Jacob [Murphy] played me through and I managed to sidestep Ezri Konsa before clipping it past Martínez. I was pleased with that one. I then had a chance to equalise in added time but after my shot was saved Alex tucked away the rebound. It finished 3-3 and was a decent start to the series for us.

MONDAY 24 JULY

"We flew back to Atlanta straight after the game so the following morning was just a case of going through our recovery programmes. Later that day we enjoyed a bit of 'team bonding' playing softball. Let's just say some of the lads were better than others! Whilst we worked very hard on the pitches or in training, downtime was also a very important part of the trip.

TUESDAY 25 JULY

"We had an open training session today and that's great for the fans to be able to see what goes on close up as it's something we're not really able to do back home. I've heard stories of how back in the Kevin Keegan days thousands of fans were able to go down to Maiden Castle and watch the likes of David Ginola and Alan Shearer. I'm sure if we were able to do that nowadays they'd turn up in their thousands too.

WEDNESDAY 26 JULY

"I was rested for the Chelsea game but what a stadium we played in. It's only about six years old but it's a real state of the art arena which even had a retractable roof and temperature control - quite incredible really. As for the game it was another good work out for us and you just knew Miggy [Almirón] would score the equaliser given he was back at his former club. The fans absolutely loved him.

THURSDAY 27 JULY

"We flew to New Jersey straight after the game given there wasn't much of a gap between our second and third games. Looking over the Hudson towards Manhattan was an incredible sight and we were delighted to get a bit of free time in the city before we left. More about that on Saturday's diary entry below.

FRIDAY 28 JULY

"The final game of the series was against Brighton, another tough challenge. We fell behind early in the second half and were still trailing with five minutes left. I still felt we had enough going for us to at least get an equaliser. And we did! Jacob [Murphy] got the ball in the box from down the right and I managed to tuck it away at the second attempt before incredibly I got the winner a few minutes into injury time. And when you grab a late goal, you normally get put up for post-match media duties!

SATURDAY 29 JULY

"Almost done. A quieter day with just some rest and recovery from the previous night's game. But also a fabulous opportunity to have a bit of a look around before going home. Sean [Longstaff], Nick [Pope] and I went over to Manhattan and spent the afternoon in Times Square which is quite an incredible place, so vibrant and buzzing. We could see the Empire State Building as well which of course is one of New York's most iconic landmarks.

SUNDAY 30 JULY

"End of the tour, pretty exhausting but all in all a fabulous trip. Breakfast at the hotel then off to the airport for the late morning flight but of course taking into account the time difference, it was just after 10 in the evening that we finally touched down in Newcastle. Straight home and off to bed, but relishing the thought of the Sela Cup the following weekend and then of course the start of the season against Aston Villa – and how good was that game! I'll sign off with another great memory of the trip, scoring the winner against Brighton in New Jersey."

QUIZ

What do you remember about the 2022/23 season?

1. Who was Newcastle's last game of 2022 against?
A) Leeds B) Chelsea C) Crystal Palace

2. United scored five goals away from home against which team?
A) Leicester B) Wolves C) West Ham

3. Who was the only outfield player to be sent off?
A) Joelinton B) Fabian Schär C) Bruno Guimarães

4. Who didn't score a penalty for Newcastle?
A) Callum Wilson B) Chris Wood C) Miguel Almirón

5. Who were the first team to beat Newcastle?
A) Arsenal B) Man Utd C) Liverpool

6. Who knocked Newcastle out of the FA Cup?
A) Burnley B) Sheffield Wednesday C) Derby

7. Who did Newcastle not beat on their way to the Carabao Cup Final?
A) Bournemouth B) West Ham C) Leicester

8. How many goals did Callum Wilson score?
A) 13 B) 18 C) 21

9. How many 0-0 draws did United have in the League?
A) One B) Four C) Seven

10. Who was the only player to make a maximum of 38 League appearances?
A) Kieran Trippier B) Nick Pope C) Sean Longstaff

And United past?

1. Who didn't score a hat-trick on their home league debut?
A) Malcolm Macdonald B) Alan Shearer C) Mick Quinn

2. In which year did Newcastle not win the FA Cup?
A) 1924 B) 1932 C) 1950

3. United signed Fabian Schär from which Spanish club?
A) Real Betis B) Deportivo de La Coruña C) Villarreal

4. United played in consecutive FA Cup Finals in the 1990s, which years?
A) 1994 & 1995 B) 1996 & 1997 C) 1998 & 1999

5. Who scored three goals for United in the 1969 Fairs Cup Final?
A) Wyn Davies B) Bob Moncur C) Bryan Robson

6. Which of these players wasn't a goalkeeper?
A) Gary Kelly B) Mike Hooper C) Scott Sellars

7. The current East Stand was opened in which year?
A) 1973 B) 1981 C) 1992

8. United's record victory against Newport County in 1946 was by what scoreline?
A) 13-0 B) 11-1 C) 14-3

9. Alan Shearer started his career at which club?
A) Blackburn B) West Ham C) Southampton

10. Who became United manager after Kevin Keegan left in 1997?
A) Bobby Robson B) Kenny Dalglish C) Ruud Gullit

NEWCASTLE UNITED

A TITLE WINNING SEASON

Newcastle United Women started the 2022/23 campaign with a lot of promise, having fallen agonisingly short of the FA Women's National League Division One North title just one season prior.

An influx of arrivals came to the club during the summer, with the likes of Daisy Burt, Freya Bailes and Charlotte Potts emerging as key starters for the Magpies throughout the course of the campaign.

Newcastle started the league as they meant to go on with a successful 4-1 away victory at Merseyrail Ladies on the opening weekend.

New summer signing Ellie Dobson made the desired impact off the bench to put the result beyond doubt for Becky Langley's team, ensuring United began the season with three points.

After following up the win over Merseyrail with a 2-0 home triumph over Stockport County at Kingston Park Stadium, Langley's team suffered their first defeat. A hard-fought clash with Hull City Ladies at home saw the visitors emerge narrow 4-3 winners, putting a dent in Newcastle's perfect start to the campaign.

Superb performances then followed, with an important win against North East rivals Middlesbrough in the league and a massive 9-1 triumph away to Lincoln City Women in the FAWNL Cup.

Durham Cestria started the campaign in a similar fashion to Newcastle and would later become the Magpies' fiercest title rivals across the campaign, enjoying successive victories over the Magpies during October.

The Wildcats eliminated Langley's side from the FAWNL Cup and inflicted the second league defeat of the season on Newcastle soon after, edging Langley's team 2-1 at Maiden Castle.

November would bring two further domestic successes, wins away at York City Ladies and Hull City in the FA Cup, before the Magpies returned to St. James' Park. The 'cathedral on the hill' was the venue, and the Vitality Women's FA Cup was the competition, with Barnsley Women going head-to-head for a place in the second round.

NEWCASTLE UNITED

HOWAY THE LASSES

28,565 supporters - a new record for the competition outside the final - packed into St. James' Park to watch the highly anticipated clash, with screamers from Georgia Gibson and Sharna Wilkinson overturning Barnsley's one-goal lead to send them to the next stage.

Despite the Magpies being eliminated from the FA Cup in the third round, after being defeated 5-1 at home by Wolverhampton Wanderers Women, Newcastle followed it up with a superb 9-0 victory over Merseyrail.

Five consecutive wins followed, with Stockport County, Chorley Women, York, Middlesbrough and Leeds all being put to the sword, before United's top-of-the-table clash with Durham Cestria.

The stage was set for a tense match under the lights at Kingston Park between the rivals, and it did not disappoint.

A cagey affair was settled by Katie Barker forcing one of the visiting players to put through her own goal, meaning the pendulum of the title race had swung in the favour of Langley and her side. The win, despite the games in hand Newcastle had on Cestria, meant that if the Magpies won every remaining match of the season, they would become champions.

At the beginning of April, the campaign's conclusion came into view, with five games standing between Newcastle and promotion. Following a 2-2 draw away at Hull, United's second St. James' Park fixture of the season was upon them. Bradford City were the visitors this time, and the Magpies put on a show for the 24,000-plus fans in attendance. Beth Guy and Potts both scored braces, while Gibson and Rachel Lee both got on the scoresheet as United eclipsed the visitors 6-1.

Three games remained, with the title still very much a possibility for Langley's team.

Due to Newcastle's superior goal difference, the task was clear: win the final three fixtures to gain promotion to the third tier.

Massive 5-1 and 6-0 away victories at Leeds and Bradford followed, setting up a final-day clash at Barnsley. Durham Cestria were playing away at Chorley on the final day, ten adrift of Newcastle in terms of goal difference. At the same time as Langley's side's match, Durham emerged 8-0 winners in their fixture, meaning just three points were between Newcastle and the title.

Kacie Elson eased nerves with her finish from Erin Nelson's cross before the break, but as the match wore on, those nerves slowly started to build once more.

Then, with just minutes remaining, Barker hammered home from within the box to prompt ecstasy among the Newcastle players, staff and fans. The pitch was swarmed and celebrations followed, topping a remarkable campaign that saw the Magpies promoted to tier three and the Northern Premier League.

To celebrate the success, Newcastle Women held a magical gala dinner attended by co-owners Amanda Staveley and Mehrdad Ghodoussi, honouring the best players from the first team and development team. The accolades didn't stop there either, with captain Grace Donnelly and Bianca Owens being honoured by the FAWNL, receiving the Golden Glove and Best Player awards for the FAWNL Division One North.

was backed up by success in cup competitions. At the end of March, the development team took part in their first final, defeating Portsmouth Ladies 3-0 at the ARMCO Arena in Solihull to lift the FA Women's National League Reserve Plate.

Langley was also recognised for her successful 2022/23, being named Best Manager for both Newcastle's division and for every single league in the FAWNL. Following her award, she said, "I am so proud to be given this award. So much work has gone into this season and I can't thank the players and staff enough.

"We strive every day to give the best representation of ourselves and inspire young girls and boys, and I hope youngsters see the success we have achieved this year and are encouraged to pursue football in the future."

But it's not just the first team that we're able to report on this year. At the beginning of the 2022/23 season, Newcastle United Women formed a development team for the very first time.

Captained by Georgina Spraggon, who was part of Newcastle's first team in 2021/22, the young Magpies ensured there was a pathway through to Langley's first team by providing a fertile environment for the young players to thrive. The likes of Jasmine McQuade and Amy Hargrave established themselves as key players for newly-appointed manager Courtney Vacher, as the development team embarked on their first-ever season in existence.

A strong league campaign, which saw Vacher's side only pipped to the title by Durham Cestria Reserves,

The young Magpies followed this up with another convincing win in the Bluefin Sport Insurance Women's Cup Final, sweeping aside West Allotment Celtic Ladies at Whitley Park.

Reflecting on the season, and her new responsibility, Spraggon spoke glowingly about the development side and what they achieved in their first campaign together.

"I think we've really pushed through and as we got to know each other as players, we started to play a lot better," she said.

"It came to the point when we knew we had the capability to go and win these things.
"Especially with that win over Portsmouth (in the FAWNL Reserve Plate Final), we went into it knowing it was going to be a difficult game but by the end, we knew we deserved to win.

"Credit to them, that's why we have done so well."

NEWCASTLE UNITED

CELEBRATIONS

The Premier League era in particular has seen a rise in the number of choreographed goal celebrations by players, not only individual ones but team ones too. You might recall the decent one performed by Bebeto and his two Brazil teammates in 1994 but in this feature we concentrate on domestic ones only, and specifically, of course, Newcastle United.

Callum Wilson scored 18 super goals in 2022/23.

Another hat-trick man, Kevin Nolan against Sunderland in the 5-1 demolition.

You could always count on Obafemi Martins to be spectacular.

Shola Ameobi in the same game!

Andy Carroll after completing his hat-trick against Aston Villa in 2010.

34

Special K (Kevin Keegan) after his debut goal in 1982.

Matt Ritchie and his corner flag kicking routine.

Supermac (Malcolm Macdonald) on his home debut against Liverpool.

The one and only legendary big Al.

Dan Burn doesn't score that many but when he does…

Peruvian Nobby Solano points the way to success.

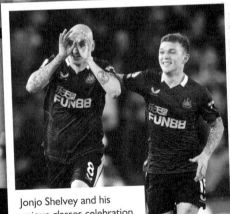
Jonjo Shelvey and his unique glasses celebration, banter with his brother.

Fingers in the ears for Spaniard Ayoze Pérez.

Ah yes, and here's that Bebeto one we referenced at the start of the feature.

Captain Bob Moncur leads the way against Újpest Dózsa in 1969.

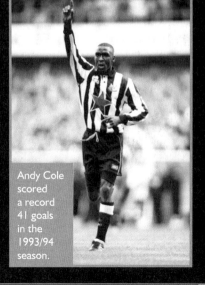
Andy Cole scored a record 41 goals in the 1993/94 season.

CARABAO CUP 2022/23

After season upon season of early round cup exits, United finally got their act together and reached their first League Cup Final since 1976 and their first Wembley final since they lost the 1999 FA Cup Final to Manchester United almost a quarter of a century ago! And it was those Red Devils who stood in the Magpies' way once again. Here's the story of how United repaired their damaged cup fighting tradition.

Round Two
Tranmere 1-2 Newcastle

The Magpies booked their passage into the Third Round after the League Two side had given them an almighty fright. The hosts opened the scoring on 21 minutes when Elliott Nevitt finished neatly before Emil Krafth was stretchered off. The Swede was replaced by Kieran Trippier and it was the England international whose corner from the right was finished by Jamaal Lascelles. Newcastle finally took control of the tie on 53 minutes when they edged ahead with a flicked header by Chris Wood, thanks to another Trippier corner.

Round Four
Newcastle 1-0 Bournemouth

United, blessed with another home draw, sealed a win against Bournemouth by virtue of an own-goal. Despite a little rustiness after a five-week hiatus due to the World Cup in Qatar, it was United who did all the attacking. Eddie Howe named a strong line-up having recalled all his World Cup stars for the tie and they did everything but score. In front of a tremendous 51,579 crowd the breakthrough came when Trippier hit a cross into the box and Adam Smith put the ball into his own net. While it was unfortunate for the Cherries, the crowd were ecstatic and the sound of Wembley songs began.

Round Three
Newcastle 0-0 Crystal Palace
(Newcastle win 3-2 on penalties)

Goalkeeper Nick Pope emerged as United's saviour when he shut out the Eagles with three spot-kick saves to help seal a 3-2 spot-kick victory which wasn't all straight-forward as both Sven Botman and Bruno Guimarães missed their kicks. Those misses were bettered by Chris Wood, Kieran Trippier and Joelinton to seal United's place in the last 16. A penalty shoot-out was the last thing Eddie Howe would have wanted as United's penalty record was abysmal at St. James' Park, but that all changed thanks to Pope's heroics between the sticks.

Quarter-Final
Newcastle 2-0 Leicester City

Goals by Dan Burn and Joelinton fired Newcastle United into the League Cup semi-finals for the first time since 1976. As the Wembley chants cascaded down from all four sides of the stadium, there was genuine cause for excitement at last. United finally came out of their shell as expectation levels rocketed with a great second-half showing. A moment Dan Burn had been waiting for all his life finally came when he took a knock-on from Joelinton and slotted the ball home before the pressure was eased when Almirón threaded a pass into Joelinton's path and the Brazilian fired home to seal the win.

Semi-Final (1st leg)
Southampton 0-1 Newcastle

No one can say United had the luck of the draw given this was the fourth tie in a row against fellow Premier League opposition. A single goal win meant if United could avoid defeat in front of a raucous St. James' Park seven days later, then they would be walking up Wembley Way to the gates of the iconic stadium. VAR ruled out a Joelinton effort but then Alexander Isak cleverly escaped his marker and crossed for Joelinton to tap in from close range. Adam Armstrong then bundled the ball home but there was a reprieve for United from VAR. Phew!

Semi-Final (2nd leg)
Newcastle 2-1 Southampton
(Newcastle win 3-1 on aggregate)

Newcastle United were going back to Wembley for the first time in 24 years. The crowd were up for it and surely Eddie Howe's side could not fail from this point. On the front foot from the first whistle, and with only four minutes on the clock, the roof almost came off when Longstaff extended United's aggregate lead. On 21 minutes United found themselves out of sight after Longstaff scored his second of the tie - cue more amazing celebrations around the stadium. Southampton reduced the arrears through Che Adams but as every second on the referee's watch ticked by, the fans were already thinking of their big day out in the capital.

Final
Manchester United 2-0 Newcastle

The Geordies turned London black and white, arriving in the capital a full 24 hours before the game and decamping in Trafalgar Square to begin the build-up. Wembley Way was the same the next day and then inside the stadium the Toon Army showed just why they are the best fans in the land bar none. And so, to the game, the Magpies had a couple of early opportunities but when the Reds hit Eddie's men with a quick two-goal salvo, through Casemiro and Rashford, United's task took on a whole more difficult look. Try as they may they couldn't get back in the game and it was a somewhat glum trip back north but at least this time the overall optimism enveloping the club meant there was much to look forward to in the weeks ahead.

COMMENTATORS CHOICE

We talk to some of the most famous voices 'behind the mic' who share the most memorable Newcastle United match they've covered during their long and distinguished careers, be it the unforgettable 5-0 thumping of Manchester United in 1996 or Craig Bellamy's last gasp winner at Feyenoord in the 2002/03 Champions League campaign.

MICK LOWES

NEWCASTLE 5-0 MANCHESTER UNITED
20 October 1996

Hot on the heels of two defeats against the Red Devils, game ten of the 1996/97 Premiership season had already been pencilled in as a red-letter day. A day of reckoning, a day for revenge. It far from disappointed. Despite beginning the match as table-toppers, defeats against Everton and Sheffield Wednesday had spluttered the start, journeys to Halmstad and Ferencváros had been agitated setbacks; this though would be United at their irresistible best. 'The Prince' was preferred at centre-back, otherwise it was full-strength, full-steam and glitteringly star-studded. The only surprise, it started with a 'scuff' before finishing with a 'scream'. Peacock's header (just),Ginola's right (bent and beyond), Ferdy's header (via a crossbar), Shearer (doing what Shearer does) and then 'The Prince'. The brilliance, the audacity, and the perfect finale. As Albert would put it a, "pièce de résistance."

STEVE WILSON

NEWCASTLE UNITED 4-4 ARSENAL
5 February 2011

Can it really be more than ten years ago? It's not every day you get to describe a 4-4 draw on BBC TV's Match of the Day programme, and I certainly haven't done it since February 2011 and that incredible day at St. James' Park. I remember afterwards that Arsenal boss Arsène Wenger was furious at how his team had collapsed once their midfielder Abou Diaby had been sent-off, and no wonder - Arsenal were winning 4-0 at the time! That red card was what got the Magpies going. Joey Barton scored two, both penalties, Leon Best got in on the act and then Cheick Tioté hammered in the equaliser at the fabled Gallowgate End with three minutes to go. The stadium literally shook; "IT'S FOUR – FOUR!", I hollered into my microphone. Well, what else could you say? And incredibly they almost got a fifth! For a while it seemed that manager Alan Pardew might be able to make Newcastle trophy contenders again. Unfortunately, that never quite happened and the memories of the game will always be tinged with sadness after Tioté - the scorer of that remarkable equaliser - died aged only 30 in 2017.

IAN DARKE

NEWCASTLE UNITED 1-0 QPR
28 August 1982

My best Newcastle memory was covering Kevin Keegan's match-winning debut for BBC Sports Report. At the time his transfer to the Toon was a sensation. He was massive news and seen as a messiah. I travelled up on the Thursday and Kevin was sitting on a wall outside the ground. He must have signed 3000 autographs. I spoke to the manager Arthur Cox and he promised me he would bring Kevin to his office at 5pm to do an interview after the Saturday game; win, lose or draw. Imagine it. Keegan got the winner against QPR. It was the only story in town. And, sure enough, Kevin walked into the manager's office bang on 5, soaking wet from the shower, wearing only a towel, to tell our listeners all about it and lead our show. It was quite a scoop for a then rather young reporter, and I loved Keegan and Cox for it.

ROGER TAMES

NEWCASTLE 7-1 LEICESTER CITY
9 May 1993

When the chairman of Newcastle United strolls on to the TV gantry at half time, picks up a microphone and starts to sing We are the Champions you realise this is a commentary that will live long in the memory. Sir John Hall had every reason to be in party mood. His team had just celebrated their pre-match coronation as runaway First Division (now The Championship) winners in a six-goal first half torrent of attacking football. With the famous old Football League trophy strangely presented before kick-off, the game was set up for a potential anti-climax. Except Kevin Keegan teams didn't do damp squibs. They did football fireworks. Hat-tricks for Andy Cole and David Kelly, another cracking goal from Rob Lee - KK's Entertainers were getting ready to take the newly formed Premier League by storm.

PETER DRURY

INTER MILAN 2-2 NEWCASTLE
11 March 2003

Perhaps - given the recent renaissance - it is fitting to pick what was, until this season, the last Champions League (proper) game Newcastle played on mainland Europe. It was wonderful. At the hotel on match day, Sir Bobby Robson invited me into the players' dining room for lunch, ostensibly (and generously) to share his team selection. But - long after the players had eaten and retreated for their afternoon nap - the great man still had me engaged in eager conversation. Instead of being ahead with my preparation, he left me chasing my tail! What a privilege!

Having scored a hat-trick in the previous European game, Alan Shearer hit two here, against the team of Zanetti, Cannavaro, Córdoba, Conceição, Di Biagio, Vieri etc. and United achieved a terrific result. The black-and-white army in the San Siro was a sight to behold. Just fabulous! Those were great days to be following The Toon… and look! Those days are coming back…

ROB HAWTHORNE

NEWCASTLE 2-0 WEST HAM
24 May 2015

It's an absolutely massive day at St. James' Park. Newcastle, who are one place above the relegation trapdoor at the start of play, need to beat West Ham on the final day of the season to ensure they stay in the Premier League. The atmosphere at St. James's Park is electrifying, and Moussa Sissoko's header puts them on track. But the hero of the hour is the player who provides the assist, as Jonás Gutiérrez goes on to score the second. It's just two months since he returned to the team after serious illness, so there is an outpouring of emotion, along with relief, at the decisive goal that means Hull, and not Newcastle, will be relegated.

GUY MOWBRAY

NEWCASTLE 6-0 ASTON VILLA
22 August 2010

The first home game of the season after promotion back to the top-flight. It was a lovely sunny August afternoon in 2010, which is mainly memorable to me for a magnificent centre forward display from Andy Carroll. It was his first home game after being awarded the famous number 9 shirt and the pressure on him must have been immense, but he rose to the challenge superbly with a performance of power, pace and fantastic finishing. A fine way for St. James' Park to welcome back Premier League football, and to think that it all started with Villa striker John Carew smashing a penalty high over Steve Harper's crossbar at the Gallowgate End. And how the Toon Army enjoyed that!

JON CHAMPION

FEYENOORD 2-3 NEWCASTLE
13 November 2002

That night in Rotterdam was a blur. It was game six in the group stages of the Champions League with many possible permutations. Newcastle threw away what should have been a decisive lead and winning the game all over again seemed beyond them until Craig Bellamy's 92nd minute intervention. There were vast hordes of Toon fans packed into De Kuip and many more back home reliant on ITV's pictures and my commentary. You always hope to find something pithy and memorable to say at pivotal moments. All I could manage was, "Bellamy… it's in… oh, extraordinary", in a voice breaking with the strain of conveying a moment of Champions League history (qualifying after losing their first three games) after 90 plus draining minutes. I still squirm when I hear it, but I guess it reflected the mood.

CLIVE TYLDESLEY

NEWCASTLE UNITED 2-0 TOTTENHAM
11 April 1999

If I am totally honest, the greatest Newcastle game I ever commentated on was the famous 4-3 defeat at Anfield in 1996 but you don't want to hear about that, do you?! Martin can have that one. Three years later I was lucky enough to have a microphone in my hand when Alan Shearer crashed an unstoppable shot into the Tottenham Hotspur net via a shuddering cross-bar at the Stretford End of Old Trafford. It sent Newcastle back to Wembley for a second successive FA Cup Final. That April afternoon in Manchester, the Stretford End was the Gallowgate End. It had been taken over by a Toon Army that were enduring a difficult season under Ruud Gullit's management. But when you've got Shearer, anything is possible. Big Al scored the first from the penalty spot before thumping home the late clincher and cueing me to shout, "that's the way to finish it, that's how he dreamt it last night".

MARTIN TYLER

LIVERPOOL 4-3 NEWCASTLE UNITED
3 April 1996

This game was not only the best Newcastle match on which I have commentated but also in my long career I regard it as the best ever! Both clubs were going for the Premier League title though neither would win it. The Magpies went a goal down in the second minute through Robbie Fowler, but Les Ferdinand equalised eight minutes later. And then the flamboyant David Ginola swept Newcastle in front - all inside the first quarter of an hour! The cut and thrust went on throughout the match. 2-2 - Fowler again, but almost immediately Faustino Asprilla struck back - 2-3 - before two sharp finishes from Stan Collymore gave Liverpool the points, his second and decisive goal in added time. Manager Kevin Keegan slumped over the advertising boards at that crucial moment of defeat, but his Entertainers had played a huge part in a truly unforgettable game.

JOHN MOTSON

HEREFORD UNITED 2-1 NEWCASTLE UNITED
5 February 1972

What an occasion this was but of course, for Newcastle United, for all the wrong reasons. I was just starting out in the television broadcasting industry and the BBC sent me down to Edgar Street to cover this FA Cup replay after the two teams had somewhat surprisingly drawn the first game at St. James' Park. No one was expecting anything but a comfortable Newcastle victory and as such a two-or-three-minute slot at the end of Match of the Day later that evening, but how wrong we all were. The game had been

postponed two or three times due to waterlogging so when we eventually got going the pitch was very heavy. Malcolm Macdonald headed Newcastle ahead late in the game and I thought that was it but then, sensationally, Ronnie Radford fired in that thunderbolt to equalise and they went on to win it in extra time through Ricky George, a goal that's often forgotten due to Ronnie's wonder goal. The fans were hanging out of the trees trying to get a vantage point and the pitch invasions (which you can't condone, of course) will be etched in the memory forever. What a day - and it set me off on many more wonderful years in the commentary box. Written by John before his sad passing in February 2023.

JOHN MURRAY

NEWCASTLE 4-1 STOKE CITY
16 January 2008

Whenever anyone asks me what makes Newcastle United different, I remember this night. It was just after I arrived in the city centre on matchday that it was confirmed. He (Kevin Keegan) was coming back. I remember thinking this is what it must have been like in some far away dictatorship after a coup when the leader of The Popular Front has returned from exile. Geordies were actually dancing in the streets. And, during the match, when the doors opened and he walked in, it was like Elvis was reborn. Of course, it went rather sour very quickly, but it was worth it for that one incredible night of Special K. Oh, and by the way, perhaps incidentally, Newcastle turned it on that night, beating their helpless opponents, rabbits caught in beaming headlights, emphatically.

IAN CROCKER

NEWCASTLE 2-1 SOUTHAMPTON
31 January 2023

I chose this match not because it was a magnificent game of football but because of the big prize that was on offer. A Wembley Cup Final. Even though Newcastle held a 1-0 lead from the first leg you could feel the tension and apprehension around St. James' Park. Local hero Sean Longstaff calmed things down with a couple of early goals but then Southampton scored and there were lingering doubts again despite a 3-1 aggregate lead. Stay calm? No chance. Newcastle doesn't do calm. If the atmosphere was mostly intense the relief was immense as reality hit home in the final few minutes. Cue one big Geordie party in that iconic arena and around that wonderful city. The wait for a trophy may go on but it's going to be a fantastic journey towards one. Enjoy the ride.

EUROPEAN NIGHTS

European nights are back at St. James' Park for the 2023/24 season, for the first time since 2012/13, and in this wonderful montage we're showcasing some of those magical 'under the lights' matches that have that extra special meaning on Tyneside since the first one against Feyenoord back in September 1968. We've also dropped in a few pictures of United on their travels.

Bobby Robson addresses his players in the Camp Nou in March 2003.

Wyn Davies in high-flying action against Sporting Lisbon at St. James' Park in November 1968.

Crunch time in Zagreb in August 1997 as Tino Asprilla prepares to take a penalty to put United ahead. He scores!

United walk out in Budapest against Ferencváros in October 1996.

A Geordie invasion of Turin in October 2002 as United take on Italian giants Juventus.

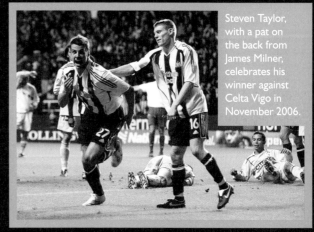

Steven Taylor, with a pat on the back from James Milner, celebrates his winner against Celta Vigo in November 2006.

United and Benfica prepare to do battle at St. James' Park in April 2013.

Supporters of United and Athletic Bilbao mingle together as they head up to the Estadio San Mamés in November 1994.

United and Real Zaragoza of Spain line up together before the Fairs Cup tie on Tyneside in January 1969.

The unforgettable home game with Barcelona in September 1997 when Tino Asprilla scored an incredible hat-trick.

Kieron Dyer celebrates scoring the only goal of the game against Željezničar of Sarajevo in August 2002.

Skipper Bob Moncur meets opposing Vitória Setubal captain Conceição (note the heavy snow) in March 1969.

BACK IN TYNE

NEWCASTLE UNITED

Season 2016/17 was definitely one to remember. That said it was in the Championship, which should never have been the case, but you just have to get on with it. Relegation in May 2016, despite an incredible 5-1 last day thumping of Tottenham Hotspur, had at least ended the season on a positive note so when Rafa Benítez's charges kicked off the new campaign in August, only one target was acceptable - promotion at the first time of asking, as had been the case when the Magpies went up in 2010. In our popular returning feature, Back in Tyne, four players who played a major part in that campaign chat with us about not only sealing that objective but winning the title in an 'you couldn't make it up' denouement to the season. Joining us are goalkeeper Karl Darlow (KD), captain Jamaal Lascelles (JL), defender Paul Dummett (PD) and striker Dwight Gayle (DG).

JL: It was such a disappointing end to the previous season, bar that last day, so we all felt we owed it to ourselves and the fans to get straight back up. Rafa had planted the seeds of recovery during his brief tenure at the club and we'd had a decent pre-season, winning four of our matches and drawing the other.

KD: I'd played in the last eight games of the 2015/16 season and, as Jamaal says, the damage had been done long before Rafa came in, that said the Tottenham game was an incredible occasion. Where else in the country would over 52,000 fans turn up to see an already relegated team play their last match of the season. And I'm certain that win was a big factor in what unfolded the following year.

JL: Some players left us in the summer, Moussa [Sissoko], Andros [Townsend], Gini [Wijnaldum] and Daryl [Janmaat] and that was entirely their choice. If they didn't fancy it in the Championship then thanks for what you did for us lads but we move on with new faces taking their place.

PD: You mean the likes of Matt Ritchie and Dwight?

JL: Well, yes, but not just you two!

DG: I'd always enjoyed playing at St. James' Park because of the big crowds and tremendous atmosphere, in fact I'd scored there a couple of seasons ago for Palace in a crazy 3-3 draw, so the move made perfect sense to me as I'm sure you'll confirm Dummy.

PD: I can vouch for that Dwight. St. James' Park is an incredible place to play as you now know for yourself. Some more lads arrived around the same time, Isaac [Hayden], Ciaran [Clark], Mo [Diamé] and DeAndre [Yedlin] that I recall and that helped boost the squad for what would be a very tough 46-game campaign.

KD: Matz Sels arrived too!

DG: Ah the keeper from Belgium Karl, didn't he start the season?

KD: Well remembered Dwight, but it wasn't long before I was back and from that moment on, I never looked back.

DG: Our first game was a Friday night affair at Fulham wasn't it. And live on telly. Not the easiest of starts for us but we were the big draw in the Championship and Sky pulled the strings as far as the fixture list was concerned.

JL: You're right Dwight and they got the 'upset' they were maybe hoping for! We didn't play particularly well and got beat 1-0. Possibly a reality check that this League would be unforgiving and we'd have to earn every point on offer.

PD: The following weekend we lost at home to Huddersfield even though Dwighty scored his first goal of the season so after two games we were 21st in the League – not exactly the start we'd envisaged.

JL: Yep, not great but there was no panic. The spirit and attitude were spot on and without being over-confident, something the gaffer would never allow us to be, we were in the right mood for the visit of Reading the following Wednesday night.

KD: That's right and watching from the bench it was a much-improved display that saw us score four against them. As was the win the following weekend, 1-0 at Bristol City when Dwight scored early on and we held on for maximum points without any real scares.

DG: Personally I was delighted to have scored four in four games but you know me lads, points before personal gratification, that's always been my motto.

JL: We ended the month with a game against Brighton, one of the teams that had made a good start and we knew would be there or thereabouts come the end of the season.

PD: I'm sure you just mentioned that because you scored!

JL: Well someone has to help you forward lads from time to time.

PD: Jonjo, one of the lads who stayed after relegation, scored a cracking free-kick to make it 2-0 and we were definitely a better team with him in it. He's never rushed and has a calming influence on everyone around him.

KD: Looks to me like he can spray passes all over the pitch with consummate ease.

DG: We had two games on the road next up and we felt if we got four or six points from them we'd really be up and running. We beat Derby 2-0 with DeAndre scoring late on.

KD: Don't mention his dress sense Dwight!

DG: I won't. And then we hit QPR for six at Loftus Road which was an absolutely stunning result. I missed that game...

PD: Is that why we scored six?

DG: But if you let me finish, I was going to add that there were some great goals that night but none better than Jonjo's 30-yard piledriver into the top corner.

JL: Many people say they don't pay much attention to the League tables but that's really a bit of a myth. We knew we were in second place and just had to keep plugging away. A cliché maybe but never more true.

PD: I remember Christian Atsu made his debut for us that night and you could never have met a more lovely lad than him which made his tragic death earlier this year even more heart-breaking.

DG: We then only took one point from the next two games and then, when we found ourselves 3-1 down to Norwich at St. James' Park with only 20 minutes to go, it was time to step up our game otherwise we'd be losing touch at the top of the table.

KD: Okay Dwight, I'll take it on from here. I was back in nets but wasn't best pleased at conceding three. You scored quite quickly after their third but five minutes into injury time we were still getting beat! Gouf [Yoan Gouffran] then equalised and we thought, well a point's not bad considering, but then when a minute later Dwight bundled in the winner, the whole place erupted.

JL: Yep, definitely a key point in the season lads.

PD: Good that you're keeping a level head skip and maintaining a sense of perspective!

DG: Christian scored his first goal for us three days later to give us the win at Rotherham and when we won the next two as well, against Brentford and Barnsley, we found ourselves in pole position.

KD: Nice word to use Dwight given the speed you drive around the place!

JL: The winning run continued into November with the key win, probably the 2-0 success at Elland Road with two opportunist goals from Dwight, especially the first one. We then lost at home to Blackburn which was an incredibly frustrating game before a second consecutive defeat at Karl and mine's former club, Nottingham Forest, followed. Now that was an injustice. Karl?

KD: It's generally always nice going back to one of your old clubs but this particular night was mad!

PD: Let me step in. Jonjo got sent-off, Karl saved a pen, Ciaran had a goal disallowed for no good reason, Matty scored, I then got sent-off and Karl saved another pen. Got it?

KD: It was crazy, at half time we felt so hard done by and obviously knew having to play the next 45 minutes two-men down was going to be incredibly difficult. The fact that they didn't get their winner until five minutes before the end, and a spawny one at that, shows how well we did. We were still top though and consolidated that with three straight wins leading up to Christmas.

DG: Wasn't Birmingham one of those games Karl?

PD: Yes, we know you scored a hat-trick Dwight, we just can't keep you down can we!

JL: The traditional Boxing Day game was as flat as they come, getting done by Sheffield Wednesday, but four days later, to end the year, we had the game we all wanted – the return fixture with Forest.

PD: To say we were up for it was an understatement. We had a score to settle and we were really buzzing when Matty knocked in a free kick after only a few minutes.

DG: Matty couldn't leave those corner flags alone could he? What have they ever done to him! By the way, didn't the fans have some sort of song about him. Something to do with a hat?

PD: Yep, it was actually a half-decent chant!

JL: Anyway, they got a man sent-off and then Dwighty got another brace and by the end of the night we were delighted with our night's work. We were a point ahead of Brighton but more importantly nine ahead of third place. Of course we would have settled for a top two place, runners-up maybe, but we're winners and that meant the Championship title was all that mattered to us.

KD: We lost at Blackburn but then won crucially at Brentford where Daryl Murphy headed the winner, He'd been around a bit but was a very nice lad and did a very effective job for us chipping in with some important goals here and there.

DG: Into January and February we kept on picking up points but it was still nip and tuck between ourselves and Brighton, they'd go top, then we would and so on. But then we reached a really pivotal part of the season. Successive games against our three main promotion rivals, all in the space of eight days and all away from home.

JL: The gaffer didn't need to instil into us the importance of this little run of games, we all knew full well how significant they were. But in his own unique way, he worked his magic and got us exactly into the right frame of mind as we travelled to Brighton for the first of the triumvirate.

PD: Glenn Murray put them ahead with an early penalty and try as we might it looked for all the world we were going to get beat. Then we fluked it, there's no other word for it. Christian mis-hit his shot and it just looped up off the heel of Mo and arched under the Brighton crossbar and into the net. Unbelievable, bizarre, call it what you want.

JL: That really shook Brighton as they could have gone four points clear with the win but when Ayoze (Pérez) scored again in the last minute, and I have to say it was a half decent ball from Matt to create it, we left the south coast in an incredibly buoyant mood.

DG: I didn't play at Brighton but was back for Saturday's visit to third place Huddersfield where a win for us would keep them at bay, 11 points behind us. Matt scored a pressure penalty…

PD: I have to say he was pretty reliable from the spot.

DG: Daryl got a second and after they pulled one back to make it a bit nervy, I got an injury time third to seal things. A funny goal really as the 'keeper was miles outside of his box, having come up for a corner and I actually ended up heading it into an empty net from outside the box – I don't score many of them!

KD: We drew at Reading the following midweek to complete a very satisfactory run and were now on the home straight. Into April and Burton Albion were the visitors for what many might have assumed would be a routine home win. It was anything but.

PD: You're telling me. We got a penalty, Matty scored it, then they (the officials) decided Dwight had encroached so they gave a free kick to Burton inside their box. We couldn't believe it and none of us had ever seen anything like it before. Thankfully Matty scored again in the second half, and a pretty decent strike it was. If we hadn't won the game I don't know what would have happened after the game in terms of protests or whatever.

JL: Leeds got an injury-time leveller against us which was a bit of a sickener then after losing to Ipswich, where to be fair we all had an off day, we bounced back to beat Preston, the game that clinched promotion, and Cardiff leaving us a last day of the season encounter at home to Barnsley.

DG: We'd achieved the aim of promotion with the Preston victory and that left us all with a wide range of emotions, joy, huge delight, pride, relief even, maybe more, but there was still unfinished business – getting our hands on the Championship trophy.

PD: Brighton were a point ahead going into their game at Aston Villa so it was out of our hands, if they won we couldn't do anything else. And to be honest we thought they would win as Villa weren't in the best of form and were lying in mid-table. And funnily enough, for a variety of reasons, I was the only one from the four of us to actually start the final game against Barnsley, remarkably really given the number of games we had played during the season.

BACK IN TYNE

KD: I was on the bench and we knew Brighton were a goal up going into the dying minutes. Surely it was all over. Dwight had just scored our third but there was still a slightly anti-climatic feel to things. Then news permeated through, Jack Grealish had equalised. Had he? Was it true? Had the game finished?

JL: Yes it was true and after an anxious few minutes when we were all on tenterhooks waiting for the final whistle at Villa Park, the scoreline was confirmed and we were Champions.

PD: We were absolutely ecstatic and the crowd, who'd played their part fantastically well during the season, exploded with unbridled joy as we all did. The trophy presentation ceremony was chaotic, but fun, and will be etched into our minds forever and the party had only just begun.

Thanks lads, that's a brilliant recollection of what was a very memorable season for the four of you and the club.

TOP 12 GOALS

We take a look back at some of the best goals from the 2022/23 season.

FABIAN SCHÄR
v Nottingham Forest
at St. James' Park, 6 August 2022

United kicked off the season on a lovely summer's afternoon (aren't there some famous song lyrics like that!) which was ignited with a typically wonderful long-range strike from Fabian Schär. Just before the hour, a clearing defensive header dropped into an area of the field towards the United right just over 25 yards out. Step forward the Swiss defender who advanced past Jesse Lingard before hammering a shot past a helpless Dean Henderson via a post and into the Leazes End net. It was almost identical to his Goal of the Month effort against Burnley in February 2019.

KIERAN TRIPPIER
v Manchester City at
St. James' Park, 21 August 2022

This was one of the best free kicks you'll ever see. Nine minutes into the second half and already holding a 2-1 lead, Allan Saint-Maximin was illegally halted outside the box by John Stones at the cost of a booking. Centrally positioned, 25 yards out, Kieran Trippier and Fabian Schär both stood over the ball before the former clipped a stunning strike over the wall and into the top corner of the Gallowgate goal on the side that Ederson had chosen to cover. Absolute perfection and bedlam in the stands ensued.

ALLAN SAINT-MAXIMIN
v Wolverhampton Wanderers at
Molineux, 28 August 2022

A much-needed last minute strike kept United's unbeaten record intact. Substitutes Elliot Anderson and Jacob Murphy combined down the right, but Murphy lost the ball in trying to keep it in play out on the byline. Hee Chan Hwang sliced it clear but only to Allan Saint-Maximin outside the box, whose perfectly struck volley flew into the bottom left-hand corner of the net in front of the Stan Cullis Stand. A top-quality strike which would win the BBC Goal of the Month award.

MIGUEL ALMIRÓN
v **Fulham** at Craven Cottage, 1 October 2022

Already one goal up just after the half hour, an extended passing sequence saw the ball played across from the United right to the left and back again, until Miguel Almirón swapped passes with Bruno Guimarães on the right-hand side of the penalty area before planting a sublime left foot volley over the goalkeeper's head. Stunning agility and a genuine 'worldie' from the Paraguayan who was in the best goal-scoring form of his career. Miggy's goal won the October BBC Goal of the Month and was also named the Premier League Goal of the Month.

CALLUM WILSON
v **Tottenham Hotspur** at Tottenham Hotspur Stadium, 23 October 2022

The deadlock was broken on 31 minutes when Fabian Schär's long ball forward dropped over Eric Dier but seemed destined to be cleared by Hugo Lloris, hence denying the lurking Wilson. Instead of putting his foot through the ball the Spurs 'keeper opted to let it bounce off his thigh, colliding with the blameless Wilson. With Lloris grounded, the ever-alert United striker turned away from goal to retrieve the ball, took a touch, and then coolly dispatched it into the unguarded net from 22 yards. Neither referee Jarred Gillett or VAR official Stuart Attwell saw anything wrong and the United fans celebrated with gusto at the opposite end of the ground.

JOE WILLOCK
v **Chelsea** at St. James' Park, 12 November 2022

The last game before the World Cup and a very important one to win. With only 23 minutes left Joelinton hooked the ball forward to Miguel Almirón, overlapping down the right. His first touch was a cushioning header before embarking on a trademark run infield across the box. Reaching halfway near the 'D', Joe Willock then appeared to whip the ball off his toes with a gorgeous powerful side-footer into the top right-hand corner of the Gallowgate net giving Édouard Mendy no chance. Wow!

ALEXANDER ISAK
v West Ham United at The London Stadium, 5 April 2023

Already cruising at 3-1 up, this goal makes the top 12 purely for its nonchalance. Good persistence from Anthony Gordon led to Schär then finding Bruno who spotted Alexander Isak moving upfield. His excellent long ball forward saw the striker stride over halfway with the figure of goalkeeper Łukasz Fabiański fast appearing, way outside his box. He however succeeded only in kneeing the ball into the path of Isak, who coolly lobbed it into the unguarded goal from 30 yards out, the scorer admiring it hands-on-hips as it went in on the first bounce.

ALEXANDER ISAK
v Brentford at The Gtech Community Stadium, 8 April 2023

Another classic from the Swedish maestro. Just past the hour mark a Brentford clearance to the halfway line was reached by Mathias Jensen, who was promptly robbed by Bruno. His short first-time pass found Joelinton and he had time to push it to Wilson, lurking to the right of the box between two defenders. Carrying the ball infield, United's number 9 laid it off to Isak, whose sweetly struck first-time right-footer flew into the net beyond the grasp of David Raya. Absolutely unstoppable.

JOELINTON
v Tottenham Hotspur at St. James' Park, 23 April 2023

The first of two classic goals from this rout of Tottenham. Ahead after 61 seconds, just five minutes later Fabian Schär played a raking pinpoint pass forward to Joelinton who timed his run impeccably to elude the Spurs backline and take the ball down with a perfect first touch before rounding Lloris and tucking the ball home. Unlike the previous instance of this ploy working at West Ham earlier in the month, there was no requirement for VAR to confirm the legitimacy of the goal. A joy to watch in its simplicity but superbly executed.

ALEXANDER ISAK
v Tottenham Hotspur at St. James' Park, 23 April 2023

Goal number four! Bruno won the ball deep inside his own half and found Joe Willock on the United left. With his first touch, Willock hit an unbelievably brilliant pass forward with the outside of his right foot that fell perfectly to Isak as he made his way down the centre of the field in full flight. The Swede took it in his stride and tucked his shot beyond Lloris into the corner without further ado. For older readers, think back to Terry Hibbitt's pass at Hillsborough in 1974 and the Supermac finish.

CALLUM WILSON
v Everton at Goodison Park, 27 April 2023

Another spectacular belter from outside the box; there'd been a few of those this season! United were 2-0 up and this delicious finish put the game to bed. Fifteen minutes from time Bruno surged forward with the ball and as he fell under challenge from Idrissa Gueye, he slid a pass towards Wilson on the edge of the 'D'. The in-form frontman took a touch and span before unleashing a perfect shot into the top corner (into the proverbial postage stamp) beyond the outstretched arms of Jordan Pickford.

JACOB MURPHY
v Everton at Goodison Park, 27 April 2023

One of the greatest assists in football history, yes it was as good as that. The absolute wizardry of Alexander Isak's run down the left was straight out of Hogwarts. Isak cut back with his route to goal obstructed by three defenders and with some sublime close control he beat all three and dribbled along the byline before finding Jacob Murphy at the far post who lashed it home from a yard out. Murphy goes in the book as the scorer but it's maybe the easiest goal he'll ever score and indeed, very similar to his back-post strike four days earlier against Tottenham.

KIERAN TRIPPIER

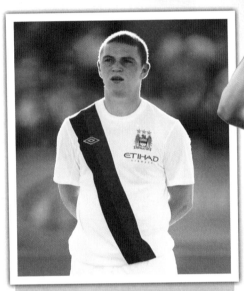

Born in Bury, Greater Manchester, Trippier began his career at nearby Manchester City, playing for their youth sides and representing England at U18, U19, U20 and U21 level. He also won the FA Youth Cup with City in 2008.

Kieran made his first steps into senior football with loan spells at Barnsley and Burnley. His loan spell with the Clarets was turned into a permanent switch in January 2012 and he helped the club to reach the Premier League in 2014, eventually clocking up four years at Turf Moor and whilst there, was named in the Championship PFA Team of the Year in consecutive seasons.

After becoming an established defender in the top-flight, he completed a move to Tottenham Hotspur in the summer of 2015 and would go on to play Champions League football at White Hart Lane, as well as making his senior debut for England against France in June 2017 - the first of 42 international caps (to the end of the 2022/23 season).

Kieran was with England at the 2018 World Cup in Russia and opened the scoring in the semi-final clash against Croatia with a stunning free-kick. Sadly, the Three Lions lost the match in extra time.

In July 2019 Kieran made a high-profile switch to Diego Simeone's Atlético Madrid, becoming the club's first English player in 95 years. In 2020/21 he made 28 league appearances as Atlético became Spanish Champions, securing the title on the last day of the season.

Kieran ended the 2020/21 campaign by starting for England in the UEFA European Championship Final at Wembley as Gareth Southgate's Three Lions narrowly lost to Italy on penalties.

In January 2022 Newcastle United confirmed the signing of the England full-back becoming the first senior signing under the club's owners and head coach Eddie Howe. Kieran linked up again with Howe after being signed by the Magpies' head coach in 2011 during his time at Burnley.

Kieran scored from two direct free-kicks in the wins over Everton and Aston Villa in February 2022 but later in the Villa game he fractured a metatarsal in his foot which kept him out of the side until the first week of May.

Back with a bang at the start of the 2022/23 season, he scored a magnificent free-kick in the home 3-3 draw with Manchester City in August. Kieran then started England's first match of the 2022 World Cup against Iran in Qatar and took the captain's armband when Harry Kane left the field.

Kieran signed a contract extension in January 2023, keeping him on Tyneside until the end of the 2024/25 season, before winning the United player of the year award for 2022/23 - a season where he started all 38 league matches.

THE NAME GAME

Paul Joannou compiles a spot of United trivia using footballer names to have played for the Magpies in senior football over the years.

SHORTEST

Demba Ba
Only two letters for the United and Senegal striker at St. James' Park between 2011 and 2012.

Sung-yueng Ki
And only two for the South Korea international who appeared in three World Cups.

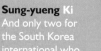

LONGEST

Zurab Khizanishvili
13 letters; almost a century of international caps for Georgia.

Keith Kettleborough
13 letters; arrived on Tyneside from Sheffield United during 1966.

JUST PERFECT

JET Milburn
Few, if any, centre-forwards can boast such a perfect set of initials as Wor Jackie; John Edward Thompson ... JET

NATIONS

Brazil
Gary; in black-and-white stripes during 1989 and 1990.

Denmark
Jimmy; Glasgow-born centre-back, 102 games for United.

Holland
Chris; joined United in 1994 as a youngster, to win ten England Under-21 caps.

Ireland
Stephen; Republic international on a brief loan period with the Magpies in 2011.

ALL VERY....
SCOTTISH

Daniel McDougal McKerrell
From Blantyre, a wartime guest who lifted the Scottish Cup.

Alexander McLeod McDougall
English not Scottish, born in Byker, with East End during the 1880s.

GREEK

Nicodemos Papavasiliou
A short stay at St. James' Park as United entered the Premier League in 1993/94.

Nikos Dabizas
Popular international centre-back who totalled 176 games for United.

FRENCH

David Desire Marc Ginola
76 classy performances for the Magpies, almost a Premier League winner.

Stéphane Pierre Yves Guivarc'h
World Cup winner with France in 1998, a £3.54m signing by United.

LATIN

Fabricio Coloccini
Argentinian international with long curly hair in 275 games.

Giuseppe Rossi
On loan with Newcastle, later winning 30 caps for Italy.

ANIMALS

Mole
George; one appearance, one goal for United back in 1900.

Hogg
Billy; celebrated Sunderland striker to guest for United in WWI.

Pigg
Albert; centre-forward at Gallowgate in the mid-20s.

Fox
Ruel; cunning on the field in attack.

FISH

Perch
James; versatile defender at Gallowgate from 2010 to 2013.

Haddock
Peter; at St. James' Park for a decade, a United fan born and bred.

BIRDS

Bird
John; tough defender of the late 1970s, later an accomplished artist.

Heron
Sam & Tom; one from 1880s and another from 1980s.

Martin
Dennis, Mick & Ian; winger, midfielder and goalkeeper, as well as another as manager.

Crowe
Charlie; FA Cup winner in 1951, born and bred in Walker.

Gavin & Darren; a pair of top-rated players at Gallowgate in the 1990s.

Swan
Chris; raised in Byker, an England youth international as he joined United during 1919.

Starling
Ron; 53 games for United then an England cap with Sheffield Wednesday.

Gosling
Dan; midfielder with Bournemouth for a lengthy spell after United.

OCCUPATIONS

Barber
Stan; Wallsend born and bred, one appearance for United then 127 for Exeter City.

Cook
John; a former soldier who played in the Northern Victory League for the Magpies.

Chandler
Bert; a handful of games when Newcastle lifted the title in 1927.

Cooper
Edward & Joe; Ed – 56 games for the black n' whites – Joe, six matches.

Farrier
Charles; another who served in World War One then played for United.

Porter
Les & Billy; two local footballers during the Second World War.

Ranger
Nile; young and controversial striker at St. James' Park from 2008 to 2013.

Shepherd
Albert; one of United's finest centre-forwards, 92 goals in 123 outings.

Turner
Arthur & Dave; played for the club 50-odd years apart.

Weaver
Sam; formidable midfielder from the Thirties, FA Cup winner and England man.

IAN DENNIS
5 Live Commentator

As a young boy my dream job was to be a football commentator and the legendary John Motson provided me with the inspiration to turn those dreams into reality.

I was a teenager when I sent him a letter asking for advice and he replied with a typed response where he said 'determination and enthusiasm' are the two attributes you will require. His words of wisdom actually apply to whatever job or career you wish to pursue, whether it be a footballer, fireman or a football commentator!

That was 1988 and 30 years on I was commentating on my first World Cup Final in Moscow which is proof that anything is possible. I had gained experience working for ClubCall, hospital radio and a bookmaker's broadcasting operation when I received my first break at the BBC in 1996 covering Durham Cricket in the north east. It was a role where I reported for Radio Cleveland and Radio Newcastle plus Look North TV, however it was short lived as Radio Newcastle offered me the Sports Editor job within months and then, within days of starting, I was dealing with the massive story that Newcastle United had signed Alan Shearer for a then world transfer record fee.

Talk about a whirlwind start!

Part of my job as Sports Editor was to commentate on Newcastle United, although I soon realised you could take nothing for granted and how precious time is when interviewing the players and manager. My first interview with Kevin Keegan was on a step in the sunshine at their old training ground in Durham and I think I was approaching close to ten minutes when the norm was nearer five minutes! Kevin walked away from me and I was not allowed to speak to him the following week! I never did that again!

He had been a dream for the media, but my first season was when he was feeling the strain and in a matter of months he had resigned. However, weeks before he left in January 1997, I was privileged to go to Lapland with Kevin Keegan, Terry McDermott and the club with 400 schoolchildren from Tyneside to visit Santa Claus on a day trip! It was -29 in Røros in northern Norway and Kevin Keegan was more popular than Santa! Special K made everybody feel so special and that really was a memorable day.

I hadn't realised at the time but covering the stories of Alan Shearer, Kevin Keegan and the appointment of Kenny Dalglish had alerted the bosses at Radio 5 and in the summer of 1998 I was invited to spend a few months working in London rather like a loan move. That year I left Newcastle for BBC Radio Leeds and then in 2002 I had joined Radio 5 on a permanent basis.

I covered different sports, read bulletins but soon focused purely on football and since 2009, when I was given the role of 'Senior Football Reporter' I have been following England and commentating on the major finals with our correspondent, John Murray.

I also commentate on the big game of the day every Saturday at 3pm which is the flagship programme on BBC Radio 5. We have almost two million listeners and millions more when the BBC World Service join to take our programme. Commentating on the game but also reading out the latest goals as they go in and handing to other reporters mean it's a fast-paced afternoon that gives me a real buzz.

I often arrive at the stadium about three hours before kick-off (and I have to say I always get very well looked after at Newcastle United) which gives me time to prepare, read my notes, read the match programme and enjoy a meal in the press room before making my way to our commentary position at about 1.30pm - still 90 minutes before kick-off. We have two positions at St. James' Park but I prefer the TV gantry in the main stand rather than the press box which is lower down behind the dug outs. It does give you an insight into how the managers feel and react during a game though. It is more open to the elements and I recall there was a match during the pandemic against Southampton and, with no cover, I was soaked to the skin before a ball had been kicked and my notes were a soggy mess!

Once the match has finished we have to be able to write a report within minutes of the final whistle to broadcast into Sports Report, or dash to the press room to interview both managers, and sometimes a player if he's made a significant input in the game, then we pack up our equipment and head home.

I feel very comfortable and familiar whenever I work at St. James' Park and it's an honour to work with the legend that is Alan Shearer. One of our favourite games was Liverpool 4 Barcelona 0 in the Champions League semi-final in 2019. An incredible comeback on a crazy night in a sensational atmosphere that we still both talk about to this day.

One funny tale is when I covered Alan Shearer's unveiling back in 1996. I was sat in the Leazes End, in amongst the fans, reporting live for Radio Newcastle. I will never forget one fan in front of me turned around and said, "Can't you get a proper job?" Politely I said nothing.

I know I'm very fortunate, but I've worked very hard in my career and it goes to show with "determination and enthusiasm" you too can achieve your dreams.

UNITED IN THE
COMMUNITY

DAN BURN SPENDS TIME WITH YOUNG HOSPITAL PATIENTS

United defender Dan Burn paid a special visit to meet children receiving treatment at the Great North Children's Hospital (GNCH) in Newcastle during Childhood Cancer Awareness Month.

Burn took time out to get to know young people and their families spending time on GNCH's paediatric oncology wards who also receive respite support from Newcastle United Foundation staff on site.

EDDIE HOWE JOINS IN WITH NEWCASTLE FOUNDATION'S WALKING FOOTBALL AND WELLBEING SESSION

Newcastle United Head Coach Eddie Howe, together with his coaching staff, attended a walking football and Football Talks session ahead of World Mental Health Day. The peer support group is attended by over 50s, with the group openly discussing a number of wellbeing issues such as social isolation and anxiety.

At the Foundation's NUCASTLE community hub, Howe and his staff took part in a walking football game competing against players who already attend the community programme.

BUILDING FOUNDATIONS AWARDS CELEBRATES NEWCASTLE UNITED FOUNDATION'S EXTRAORDINARY COMMUNITY

The inspirational achievements of North-East community members connected by Newcastle United were celebrated at Newcastle United Foundation's Building Foundations Awards ceremony which recognised the remarkable children, young people, families and older generations who have created positive change for themselves and the region.

Among 400 guests at the black-tie gala were Newcastle United directors Amanda Staveley and Mehrdad Ghodoussi, the club's CEO Darren Eales and Sporting Director Dan Ashworth, alongside representatives from the Magpies' first team, Newcastle United Women, former players, and Foundation participants.

EMIL KRAFTH MEETS FUTURE FOOTBALLERS LEARNING AT NUCASTLE WITH NEWCASTLE UNITED FOUNDATION

Emil Krafth helped inspiring young footballers develop their skills on the pitch and in the classroom alongside Newcastle United Foundation.

The Swedish defender met with pupils from North Gosforth Academy, in Newcastle, and Sävsjö school students from Sweden visiting the Foundation's new home. Krafth heard how the two school groups spent a day together as part of the Foundation's Partner School programme funded by the Premier League.

BRUNO DELIGHTS YOUNG SUPPORTERS AT NEWCASTLE UNITED FOUNDATION DISABILITY FOOTBALL SESSION

Bruno Guimarães was a surprise guest at a Newcastle United Foundation disability session where families enjoyed a free weekly Down syndrome football session at NUCASTLE.

Met with roaring cheers and chants, Bruno – joined by his father – settled straight into a game of football with teenagers and young adults before signing autographs and posing for pictures with participants. Bruno's visit marked World Down Syndrome Day, creating awareness and advocacy for the rights, inclusion and wellbeing of people with Down syndrome.

ANTHONY GORDON HAS A KICKABOUT WITH REFUGEES, MIGRANTS AND PEOPLE SEEKING SANCTUARY AT NEWCASTLE UNITED FOUNDATION

Anthony Gordon delighted dozens of recently arrived refugees, migrants and young people seeking sanctuary when he spent an afternoon getting to know Newcastle United Foundation's community.

Joining in with a football game, Gordon spent time meeting and chatting to participants from all over the world who are making a new home and a new life for themselves in the North-East. The Foundation's Welcome Through Football programme provides a unique opportunity to assist the integration through a shared passion for football.

Gordon hailed the Foundation's "incredible" work and facilities which are available for all community members to enjoy.

SEAN LONGSTAFF SUPPORTS ENVIRONMENTAL SUSTAINABILITY

Ahead of Earth Day, midfielder Sean Longstaff took part in a sustainability lesson at Newcastle United Foundation, learning from a group of pupils who are set to represent the club's charity as they compete in a national competition.

Sean, an Ambassador for Newcastle United Foundation, learnt about the impact of climate change and met with pupils from Duke's Secondary School, whose winning idea on the sustainability project was to reuse old pallets from St. James' Park and transform them into 'birdboxes' and 'bug hotels' to increase natural habitats and improve biodiversity, with the recycled boxes being housed along the wildlife corridor between the club's Training Centre and Academy.

NEWCASTLE UNITED FOUNDATION INSPIRE NEXT GENERATION WITH NEWCASTLE UNITED WOMEN ON INTERNATIONAL WOMEN'S DAY

Young women and girls aspiring towards a future in football with Newcastle United Foundation have learned "the sky's the limit" while meeting their heroes from Newcastle United Women.

To honour International Women's Day, the Magpies' Daisy Burt and Cara Milne-Redhead created an inspirational training session for players involved in the Foundation's Emerging Talent Centre.

Burt and Milne-Redhead saw first-hand how the next generation are gearing up towards a career in women's football at an ETC training session on the rooftop pitch at the Foundation's community facility.

Q&A

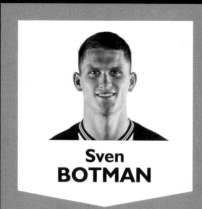
Sven BOTMAN

Katie BARKER

	Sven BOTMAN	Katie BARKER
DESCRIBE YOURSELF IN THREE WORDS	Sporty, happy, handsome!	Competitive, committed, fast
HERO GROWING UP	Cristiano Ronaldo	Lionel Messi
BEST FOOTBALLING MOMENT	Winning the league with Lille in 2020/21	Being the first woman to score a competitive goal at SJP (against Alnwick in 2022)
TOUGHEST OPPONENT	Neymar	Charlotte Potts in training!
TEAM SUPPORTED AS A YOUNGSTER	Real Madrid	Newcastle United
PRE-MATCH MEAL	Pancakes	Home game – beans on toast Away game – pasta
SUPERSTITIONS	Put my left boot on first	None
FAVOURITE CURRENT PLAYER	Luka Modrić	Lionel Messi
FAVOURITE OTHER SPORTS PERSON	Rafa Nadal	LeBron James
FAVOURITE STADIUM OTHER THAN SJP	The Bernabéu	Nou Camp, Barcelona
PERSONAL HIGHLIGHT OF 2022/23 SEASON	Getting a ticket for the Carabao Cup Final!	Scoring the second goal at Barnsley on the last day of the season to help secure the league title
WHAT WOULD YOU BE IF YOU WEREN'T A FOOTBALLER	A property seller	Jeff Stelling (i.e. a TV pundit!)
FAVOURITE HOLIDAY DESTINATION	Mykonos	Lanzarote
IF YOU COULD CHANGE ONE THING ABOUT FOOTBALL, WHAT WOULD IT BE	VAR not taking absolutely ages	Replace throw-ins with kick-ins
WHAT ARE YOU LOOKING FORWARD TO MOST IN 2023/24	Hopefully winning something with Newcastle	My first full season as a professional and Champions League nights

Alexander ISAK	Kacie ELSON	Joe WILLOCK
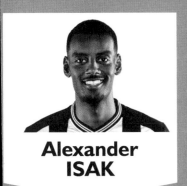		
Relaxed, competitive, dedicated	Confident, determined, funny	Shy, retiring, modest
Lionel Messi	David Beckham	Thierry Henry
Winning the cup in Spain with Real Sociedad	Winning the 2022/23 FAWNL and gaining promotion	Making my Arsenal debut aged 17
Sergio Ramos	Not an opponent but a team – Wolverhampton Ladies FC in the FA Cup	Paul Pogba
AIK Stockholm	As a youngster it was Manchester United, but now it's Newcastle!	Arsenal
Rice and salmon	Chicken, vegetables and rice, or chicken pasta	Penne pasta
Put my right boot on first	I have to wear two certain types of socks	White tape on my left wrist
Sven Botman	Jack Grealish, however I have always idolised Cristiano Ronaldo	Chris Willock (my brother who's at QPR)
LeBron James	Serena Williams	Serena Williams
The Bernabéu	Wembley	Mercedes-Benz (Atlanta)
Scoring on my debut at Anfield	Scoring the first goal in the final game of the season, it meant so much to us all	Qualifying for the Champions League with the lads
An astronaut	A sports finance advisor or contract negotiator	Scientist
The Greek Islands	America	Too many to mention!
Make the offside rule favour the attacker more	Players having to go off after treatment, the player who committed the foul should go off instead so the injured player's team isn't disadvantaged	Social media
Scoring goals for Newcastle	Playing professionally and building upon the momentum from 2022/23	Champions League

QUIZ ANSWERS

Page 17: Spot the Ball:

Page 20: Spot the Difference

Page 29: Quiz

2022/23 Season		United Past	
1.	Leeds	1.	Alan Shearer
2.	West Ham	2.	1950
3.	Bruno Guimarães	3.	Deportivo de La Coruña
4.	Miguel Almirón	4.	1998 & 1999
5.	Liverpool	5.	Bob Moncur
6.	Sheffield Wednesday	6.	Scott Sellars
7.	West Ham	7.	1973
8.	18	8.	13-0
9.	Seven	9.	Southampton
10.	Kieran Trippier	10.	Kenny Dalglish